Sip! Sip! Sip!

By Cameron Macintosh

Sam sits at the mat.

Sam sips!

mat

Pam sits at the pit.

Sip, Pam, sip!

pit

Tam is at the tap.

Tam sips!

tap

I am at the tap!

Sip! Sip! Sip!

tap

CHECKING FOR MEANING

1. Where is Tam? *(Literal)*

2. Who sits at the mat? *(Literal)*

3. What might Sam and Pam be drinking? *(Inferential)*

EXTENDING VOCABULARY

pit	Look at the word *pit*. How many sounds are in the word? What other words can you think of that rhyme with *pit*?
at	Look at the word *at*. What words do you know that end in *at*?
mat	Look at the word *mat*. Can you think of another word that means the same as *mat*?

MOVING BEYOND THE TEXT

1. What might the friends do next?

2. What do you like to do with your friends?

3. What are some different things that you can drink from?

4. Do you think water is a good drink? Why or why not?

SPEED SOUNDS

| Mm | Ss | Aa | Pp | Ii | Tt |

PRACTICE WORDS

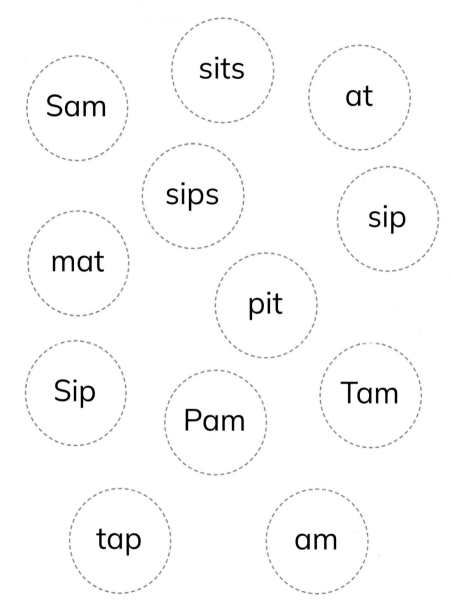

Sam

sits

at

sips

sip

mat

pit

Sip

Pam

Tam

tap

am